FABULOUS
CAKES

FABULOUS CAKES

OVER 40 GLORIOUS CLASSIC, SPECIAL OCCASION AND NOVELTY CAKES MADE SIMPLE

SARAH MAXWELL AND ANGELA NILSEN

PHOTOGRAPHY BY TIM HILL

ACROPOLIS BOOKS

Acknowledgements

The publisher and authors would like to thank Scenics Cakes Boards and Colours Direct, 081–441 3082, and the Cloth Store, 0293 560943, for supplying props and materials; Braun and Kenwood for the use of their equipment; Stork Cookery Service for the Rich Fruit Cake chart and Jackie Mason for her help.

First published in 1994 by Lorenz Books

© 1994 Anness Publishing Ltd

Lorenz Books is an imprint of
Anness Publishing Limited
1 Boundary Row
London SE1 8HP

This edition exclusively distributed in Canada by
Book Express, an imprint of Raincoast Books Distribution Limited
112 East 3rd Avenue
Vancouver
British Columbia V5T 1C8

Distributed in Australia by Treasure Press

ISBN 1 85967 039 3
A CIP catalogue record for this book is available from the British Library

Editorial Director: Joanna Lorenz
Project Editors: Judith Simons and Clare Nicholson
Photographer: Tim Hill
Home Economists: Sarah Maxwell and Angela Nilsen
Assistant Home Economist: Teresa Goldfinch
Stylist: Sarah Maxwell
Assistant Stylist: Timna Rose
Design: Axis Design
Jacket Design: Peter Butler

Printed and bound in Singapore

Contents

Introduction 7

Classic Cakes 9

Special Occasion Cakes 31

Children's Party Cakes 53

Basic Cakes 82

Basic Icings 89

Index 96

Introduction

The fabulous cakes in this book are divided into three, equally imaginative, sections. The first contains a fine selection of classic cakes, ranging from the German Battenberg to a traditional rich chocolate creation. This is followed by a chapter devoted to really beautiful cakes, each for a special occasion such as New Year, St Valentine's Day or a birthday. Then comes the children's party cakes – truly creative, they include a clown and a magic carpet complete with the genie of the lamp.

Finally, many of these recipes feature standard cake mixes, such as quick-mix sponge and rich fruit cake, and icings, such as marzipan and sugarpaste. Where this is the case, the mix or icing appears at the end of the book in the chapter on basic cakes and basic icings. This section tells you exactly how to make each cake and quantities are given for all the shapes and sizes included in the recipes in this book.

Within each recipe all the ingredients are given in metric, imperial and cup measurements. When following a recipe, always work with one set of ingredients only as mixing them might result in disappointment. For the best results, use eggs which are at room temperature, and sift flour after you have measured it. If you sift the flour from a fair height, it will have more chance to aerate and lighten.

No two ovens are alike. Buy a reliable oven thermometer and test the temperature of your oven. When possible, bake in the centre of the oven where the heat is more likely to be constant. If using a fan assisted oven, follow the manufacturer's guidelines for baking. Good quality cake tins can also improve your results, as they conduct heat more efficiently.

Whatever the occasion, whatever the cake, this book will guarantee you cakes which not only look good – they taste great too.

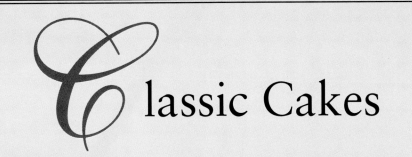

Classic Cakes

Classic Cakes includes traditional favourites, perfect for teas, picnics, and formal and informal gatherings. Battenberg, Shortcake, Dundee cake, Roulade, Chocolate gâteau, Madeira cake and many more are included, sometimes in their classic form and sometimes excitingly reinterpreted for this book.

Crunchy-topped Madeira Cake

*Traditionally served with a glass of Madeira
wine in Victorian England, this light sponge still makes
a perfect tea-time treat.*

INGREDIENTS
Serves 8–10
200 g/7 oz/14 tbsp butter, softened
finely grated zest of 1 lemon
150 g/5 oz/³/₄ cup caster sugar
3 size 3 eggs
75 g/3 oz/³/₄ cup plain flour, sifted
150 g/5 oz/1¼ cups self-raising
flour, sifted

For the Topping
3 tbsp clear honey
115 g/4 oz/³/₄ cup plus 2 tbsp
chopped mixed peel
50 g/2 oz/¹/₂ cup flaked almonds

STORING
*This cake can be kept for up to
three days in an airtight container.*

1 Preheat the oven to 180°C/350°F/
Gas 4. Grease a 450 g/1 lb loaf tin,
line the base and sides with greaseproof
paper and grease the paper.

2 ▲ Place the butter, lemon zest and
sugar in a mixing bowl and beat
until light and fluffy. Beat in the eggs,
one at a time, until evenly blended.

3 ▲ Sift together the flours, then stir
into the egg mixture. Transfer the
cake mixture to the prepared tin and
smooth the surface.

4 ▲ Bake in the centre of the oven for
45–50 minutes or until a skewer
inserted into the centre of the cake
comes out clean. Leave the cake in the
tin for about 5 minutes. Turn out on to
a wire rack, peel off the lining paper
and leave to cool completely.

5 ▲ To make the topping, place the
honey, chopped mixed peel and
almonds in a small saucepan and heat
gently until the honey melts. Remove
from the heat and stir briefly to coat the
peel and almonds, then spread over the
top of the cake. Allow to cool
completely before serving.

Gorgeous Chocolate Cake

This recipe will definitely make you famous. Make sure you serve it with paper and pens, as everyone will want to take down the recipe.

INGREDIENTS
Serves 8–10

175 g/6 oz/³/₄ cup butter, softened
115 g/4 oz/¹/₂ cup caster sugar
250 g/9 oz/9 squares plain chocolate, melted
200 g/7 oz/2¹/₃ cups ground almonds
4 size 3 eggs, separated
115 g/4 oz/4 squares white chocolate, melted, to decorate

STORING
This cake can be kept for up to four days in an airtight container.

1 Preheat the oven to 180°C/350°F/ Gas 4. Grease a deep 21 cm/8¹/₂ inch springform cake tin, then line the base with greaseproof paper and grease the paper.

2 ▲ Place 115 g/4 oz/¹/₂ cup of the butter and all the sugar in a mixing bowl and beat until light and fluffy. Add two thirds of the plain chocolate, the ground almonds and the egg yolks and beat until evenly blended.

3 ▲ Whisk the egg whites in another clean, dry bowl until stiff. Fold them into the chocolate mixture, then transfer to the prepared tin and smooth the surface. Bake for 50–55 minutes or until a skewer inserted into the centre of the cake comes out clean. Leave the cake in the tin for about 5 minutes, then turn out on to a wire rack, peel off the lining paper and leave to cool completely.

4 ▲ Place the remaining butter and remaining melted plain chocolate in a saucepan. Heat very gently, stirring constantly, until melted. Pour over the cake, allowing the topping to coat the sides too. Leave to set for at least an hour. To decorate, fill a piping bag with the melted white chocolate and snip the end. Drizzle all around the edges to make a double border. Use any remaining chocolate to make leaves (see Trailing Orchid Wedding cake, steps 2 and 3).

Tip

Place a large sheet of greaseproof paper or a baking sheet under the wire rack before pouring the chocolate topping over the cake. This will catch all the drips and keep the work surface clean.

utumn Passionettes

Perfect for a tea party or packed lunch, this passion cake mixture can also be made as one big cake to serve for a celebration or as a dessert.

INGREDIENTS
Makes 24
150 g/5 oz/³/₄ cup butter, melted
200 g/7 oz/⁷/₈ cup soft light brown sugar
115 g/4 oz/1 cup carrots, peeled and finely grated
50 g/2 oz/1 cup dessert apples, peeled and finely grated
pinch of salt
1–2 tsp ground mixed spice
2 size 3 eggs
200 g/7 oz/1³/₄ cups self-raising flour
2 tsp baking powder
115 g/4 oz/1 cup shelled walnuts, finely chopped

For the Topping
175 g/6 oz/³/₄ cup full-fat soft cheese
4–5 tbsp single cream
50 g/2 oz/¹/₂ cup icing sugar, sifted
25 g/1 oz/¹/₄ cup shelled walnuts, halved
2 tsp cocoa powder, sifted

STORING
Both the large and small cakes can be kept for up to four days in an airtight container.

1 Preheat the oven to 180°C/350°F/ Gas 4. Arrange 24 fairy cake paper cases in bun tins and put to one side.

2 ▲ Place the butter, sugar, carrots, apples, salt, mixed spice and eggs in a mixing bowl and beat well to combine.

3 ▲ Sift together the flour and baking powder into a small bowl, then sift again into the mixing bowl. Add the chopped walnuts and fold in until evenly blended.

4 ▲ Fill the paper cases half-full with the cake mixture, then bake for 20–25 minutes, or until a skewer inserted into the centres of the cakes comes out clean.

5 Leave the cakes in the tins for about 5 minutes, before transferring them to a wire rack to cool completely.

6 ▲ To make the topping, place the full-fat soft cheese in a mixing bowl and beat in the cream and icing sugar until smooth. Put a dollop of the topping in the centre of each cake, then decorate with the walnuts. Dust with sifted cocoa powder and allow the icing to set before serving.

Tip

To make one big cake, which will serve 6–8, grease a 20 cm/8 inch fluted American bundt cake tin and line the base with greaseproof paper. Grease the paper. Place all of the cake mixture in the tin and bake for about 1¼ hours, or until a skewer inserted into the centre of the cake comes out clean. Leave the cake in the tin for about 5 minutes. Turn out on to a wire rack, peel off the lining paper and leave to cool completely. Decorate with the topping mixture, walnuts and sifted cocoa powder.

Jazzy Chocolate Gâteau

This cake is made with Father's Day in mind, though really it can be made for anyone who loves chocolate.

INGREDIENTS
Serves 12–15
2 x quantity chocolate-flavour
Quick-Mix Sponge Cake mix
75 g/3 oz/3 squares plain chocolate
75 g/3 oz/3 squares white chocolate
½ quantity Fudge Frosting
½ quantity Glacé Icing
1 tsp weak coffee
8 tbsp chocolate hazelnut spread

MATERIALS AND EQUIPMENT
2 x 20 cm/8 inch round cake tins
greaseproof paper piping bag
No 1 writing nozzle

STORING
The finished cake can be kept for up to three days in the fridge.

1 Preheat the oven to 160°C/325°F/ Gas 3. Grease the cake tins, line the bases with greaseproof paper and grease the paper. Divide the cake mixture evenly between the tins and smooth the surfaces. Bake in the centre of the oven for 20–30 minutes, or until firm to the touch. Turn out on to a wire rack, peel off the lining paper and leave to cool completely.

2 Meanwhile, cover a large baking sheet or board (or two smaller ones) with baking parchment and tape it down at each corner. Melt each chocolate in separate bowls over pans of hot water, stirring until smooth, then pour on to the baking parchment. Spread out the chocolates evenly with a palette knife. Allow to cool until the surfaces are firm enough to cut, but not so hard that they will break. The chocolate should no longer feel sticky when touched with your finger.

3 ▲ Cut out haphazard shapes of chocolate and set aside.

4 ▲ Make the fudge frosting and, when cool enough to spread, use to sandwich the two cakes together. Place the cake on a stand or plate.

5 Make the glacé icing, using 1 tsp weak coffee (to colour it very slightly) along with enough water to form a spreading consistency, and spread on top of the cake almost to the edges. Spread the side of the cake with enough chocolate hazelnut spread to cover.

6 ▲ Arrange the chocolate pieces around the side of the cake, pressing into the hazelnut spread to secure.

7 To decorate, spoon about 3 tbsp of the chocolate hazelnut spread into a piping bag fitted with a No 1 nozzle and pipe 'jazzy' lines over the glacé icing.

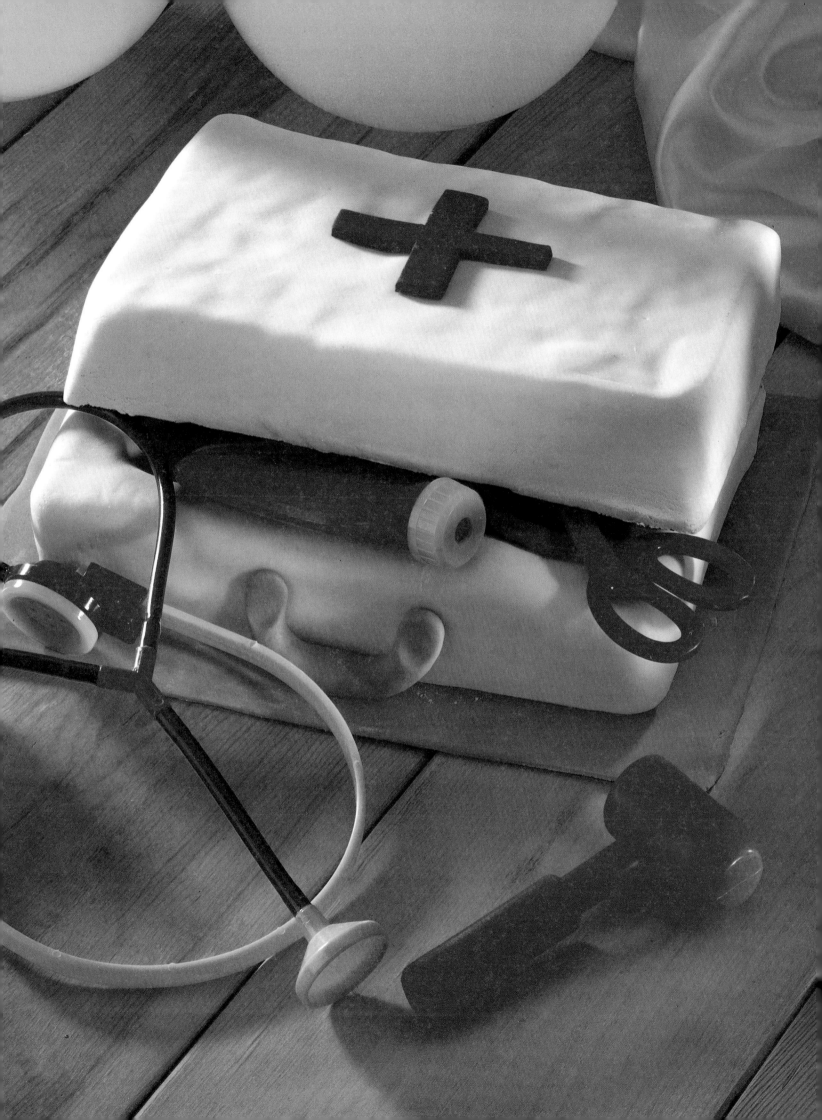

Spiders' Web Cake

A spooky cake for any occasion, fancy dress or otherwise. Put as many spiders as you like on the cake, but any leftover ones can be put on the children's plates or arranged to look like they're crawling all over the table.

INGREDIENTS

Serves 6–8
1 quantity lemon-flavour Quick-Mix Sponge Cake mix
1 quantity lemon-flavour Glacé Icing
yellow and black food colourings

For the Spiders
115 g/4 oz/4 squares plain chocolate, broken into pieces
150 ml/¼ pint/⅔ cup double cream
3 tbsp ground almonds
cocoa powder, for dusting
chocolate vermicelli
2-3 liquorice wheels, sweet centres removed
15 g/½ oz Sugarpaste Icing

MATERIALS AND EQUIPMENT
900 g/2 lb fluted dome-shaped tin or pudding basin
20 cm/8 inch cake board
small greaseproof paper piping bag
wooden skewer

STORING
The finished cake can be kept in a cool, dry place for up to two days.

1 Preheat the oven to 180°C/350°F/ Gas 4. Grease and flour the fluted dome-shaped tin or pudding basin. Spoon in the cake mixture and smooth the surface. Bake in the centre of the oven for 35–40 minutes or until a skewer inserted into the centre of the cake comes out clean.

2 ▲ Leave the cake in the tin for about 5 minutes, then turn out on to a wire rack and leave to cool completely.

3 Place about 3 tbsp of the glacé icing in a small bowl. Stir a few drops of yellow food colouring into the larger quantity of icing and colour the small quantity black. Place the cake on the cake board, dome side up, and pour over the yellow icing, allowing it to run, unevenly, down the sides. Fill the piping bag with the black icing. Seal the bag and snip the end, making a small hole for the nozzle.

4 ▲ Starting on the top of the cake, in the centre, drizzle the black icing round the cake in a spiral, keeping the line as continuous and as evenly spaced as possible. Use the wooden skewer to draw through the icing, downwards from the centre at the top of the cake, to make a web effect. Wipe away the excess icing with a damp cloth, then allow the icing to set at room temperature.

5 To make the spiders, place the chocolate and cream in a small, heavy-based saucepan and heat gently, stirring frequently, until the chocolate melts. Transfer the mixture to a small mixing bowl and allow to cool.

6 ▲ When cool, beat the mixture for about 10 minutes or until thick and pale. Stir in the ground almonds, then chill until firm enough to handle. Dust your hands with a little cocoa, then make a ball the size of a large walnut out of the chocolate mixture. Roll each ball in chocolate vermicelli until evenly coated. Repeat this process until all the mixture is used.

7 ▲ To make the spiders' legs, cut the liquorice into 4 cm/1½ inch lengths. Make small cuts into the sides of each spider, then insert the legs. To make the spiders' eyes, pull off a piece of sugarpaste icing about the size of a hazelnut and colour it with black food colouring. Use the white icing to make tiny balls and the black icing to make even smaller ones. Use a little water to stick the eyes in place. Arrange the spiders on and around the cake.

Puppies in Love

*Out of one Swiss roll come two gorgeous puppy dogs.
This cake looks extremely impressive, without
being too difficult to prepare.*

INGREDIENTS
Serves 8–10
1 quantity chocolate-flavour Swiss
Roll mix
¼ quantity chocolate-flavour
Butter Icing
115 g/4 oz yellow marzipan
green, brown, pink and red food
colourings
75 g/3 oz/1½ cups desiccated
coconut
450 g/1 lb/1⅓ x quantity
Sugarpaste Icing
4 tbsp apricot jam, warmed and
sieved

MATERIALS AND EQUIPMENT
33 x 23 cm/13 x 9 inch Swiss
roll tin
25 cm/10 inch square cake board
small round cutter
10 cm/4 inch piece of thin ribbon

STORING
The finished cake can be kept in a
cool, dry place for up to two days.

1 Preheat the oven to 180°C/350°F/
Gas 4. Grease the Swiss roll tin, line
with greaseproof paper and grease the
paper. Spoon in the cake mixture and
smooth the surface. Bake in the centre
of the oven for about 12 minutes or
until springy when touched in the
centre. Leave to cool in the tin, on a
wire rack, covered with a clean, just-
damp cloth. Then invert the cake on to
a sheet of greaseproof paper, dredged
with icing sugar.

2 Trim the edges of the cake, then
spread with the chocolate butter
icing, reserving a tiny amount. Roll up
the Swiss roll, using the greaseproof
paper as a guide, then cut in half
widthways.

3 ▲ To make the faces, cut the
marzipan in half and roll each portion
into a ball, then into a squat cone shape.
Use a little of the reserved butter icing to
stick the faces on to the bodies.

4 Place a few drops of green food
colouring in a bowl with the
desiccated coconut. Add a few drops of
water and stir until the coconut is
flecked with green and white. Scatter it
over the cake board then position the
two puppies a little apart on the board.

5 Cut off about 25 g/1 oz of the
sugarpaste icing and set aside,
wrapped in clear film. Colour half the
remaining icing brown and half pink.
Cut off about 50 g/2 oz from each
colour and wrap in clear film.

6 ▲ Lightly dust the work surface
with icing sugar and roll out the
larger portions of brown and pink
icings into 11 x 35 cm/4½ x 14 inch
rectangles. Cut in half widthways and
trim the edges. Cover all four sections
with clear film and set aside.

7 ▲ Roll out the reserved pieces of
brown and white icings, then use
the small round cutter to stamp out
several shapes. Gather up the icing
trimmings and set aside, wrapped in
clear film. Stick the white rounds on to
one of the brown rectangles, then the
brown rounds on to one of the pink
rectangles, using a little water. Use a
rolling pin to press them in slightly.

8 Use a sharp knife to slash all four
icing rectangles along the two short
edges. Brush the body of each puppy
with jam, then lay the brown icing
without spots over one body, and the
pink icing without spots over the other.
Place a little water on the back of each,
then put the brown spotty icing over the
brown dog and the pink spotty icing
over the pink dog.

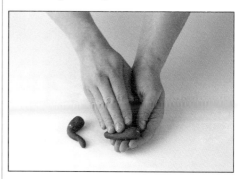

9 ▲ Roll half of the reserved icings in
your hands to make little tails. Stick
them in place with a little reserved
butter icing. Make a little fringe from
the brown icing for the brown puppy,
and tie a few strands of pink icing
together with the ribbon to make a
fringe for the pink puppy. Stick them in
place with a little water.

10 Use the remaining pieces of
sugarpaste icing to make the
facial features for each puppy, choosing
your own expressions, then stick them
in place with some water. The little
heart-shaped food bowl is an optional
extra, or you can make a small bone, if
you prefer.